THINK
LIKE
GOD

The Key to a Better Life

JOHN BLIG

WESTBOW
P R E S S®
A DIVISION OF THOMAS NELSON
& ZONDERVAN

Unless otherwise stated, scripture taken from the King James Version of the Bible.
Scripture quotations taken from the New American Standard Bible® (NASB),
Copyright © 1960, 1962, 1963, 1968, 1971, 1972, 1973,
1975, 1977, 1995 by The Lockman Foundation
Used by permission. www.Lockman.org
Scripture quotations taken from the Amplified® Bible (AMP),
Copyright © 2015 by The Lockman Foundation
Used by permission. www.Lockman.org
Scripture quotations marked (NIV) are taken from the Holy Bible, New International Version®,
NIV®. Copyright © 1973, 1978, 1984, 2011 by Biblica, Inc.™ Used by permission of Zondervan.
All rights reserved worldwide. www.zondervan.com The "NIV" and "New International Version"
are trademarks registered in the United States Patent and Trademark Office by Biblica, Inc.™
Scripture quotations marked MSG are taken from THE MESSAGE, copyright © 1993,
1994, 1995, 1996, 2000, 2001, 2002 by Eugene H. Peterson. Used by permission of
NavPress. All rights reserved. Represented by Tyndale House Publishers, Inc.
Scripture taken from the New King James Version®. Copyright © 1982
by Thomas Nelson. Used by permission. All rights reserved.
Scripture quotations from The Authorized (King James) Version. Rights in the
Authorized Version in the United Kingdom are vested in the Crown. Reproduced
by permission of the Crown's patentee, Cambridge University Press

WestBow Press books may be ordered through booksellers or by contacting:

WestBow Press
A Division of Thomas Nelson & Zondervan
1663 Liberty Drive
Bloomington, IN 47403
www.westbowpress.com
1 (866) 928-1240

Because of the dynamic nature of the Internet, any web addresses or links contained in
this book may have changed since publication and may no longer be valid. The views
expressed in this work are solely those of the author and do not necessarily reflect the
views of the publisher, and the publisher hereby disclaims any responsibility for them.

Any people depicted in stock imagery provided by Thinkstock are models,
and such images are being used for illustrative purposes only.
Certain stock imagery © Thinkstock.

ISBN: 978-1-5127-9785-5 (sc)
ISBN: 978-1-5127-9786-2 (hc)
ISBN: 978-1-5127-9784-8 (e)

Library of Congress Control Number: 2017912004

Print information available on the last page.

WestBow Press rev. date: 09/22/2017

CONTENTS

ACKNOWLEDGMENTS

First, I would like to thank God for the revelation that He keeps giving me by the Spirit of Revelation, who is the Holy Spirit, as well as for the inspiration to write this book.

I want to thank my wife, Michaela, and my children, Jason, Melody, and Harmony, for the great family environment created to enable me to write as well as the positive support and encouragement to step forward in writing.

I also want to thank all my friends, especially Oasis of Light Church, where I get to minister every Sunday and receive new revelation and inspiration from the Lord while doing that.

A special thank you to Mary Munoz from Oasis of Light Church, who worked so hard in editing this book for me.

It is such a joy to be surrounded by so many people of value, people that encourage me, help me, and bless me every step of the way.

Thank you!
John Blig

PREFACE

The purpose of this book is to give the reader a clear picture of God being a God of unconditional love, overwhelming goodness, and extravagant generosity, causing people who dare to read through this entire book to fall in love effortlessly and helplessly with the real God as well as to receive freely everything our heavenly Father has already provided for us through the life, ministry, death, and resurrection of our Lord Jesus Christ.

I have witnessed people's lives being effortlessly transformed just by listening to this message and allowing the life of our Lord Jesus Christ from within them to flow freely and to impact the people around them in a powerful way. There are a lot of scriptures quoted throughout this book because I believe that if one's mind and life are going to be transformed by anyone, that someone needs to be the Holy Spirit, the one who points us to the living Word of God, who is none other than our Lord Jesus Christ, and to the scriptures themselves.

INTRODUCTION

People read a lot of books on many different subjects. They go to school for extended periods to learn certain skills or professions; they pay large sums of money to acquire knowledge in different areas of life; and they ultimately make sacrifices in moving to other locations in order to accomplish all of this.

Now, all these endeavors are good in and of themselves, but what if we could read a book on how the one who has all knowledge, all wisdom, and all understanding thinks, the one who is absolutely the best in every field of study—that being the Holy Spirit of God, who is the best teacher that has ever existed? What if we could be trained by the creator Himself? And what if all of this was without much sacrifice and very little expense? What if we could learn how God thinks and then think like Him? After all, He is the one who has all wisdom, knowledge, and understanding.

> *Great is our Lord and abundant in strength: His understanding is infinite.*
>
> Psalm 147:5 NAS

> *For God is greater than our heart and knows all things.*
>
> 1 John 3:20 NAS

But the very hairs of your head are all numbered.

Matthew 10:30 NAS

He counts the number of the stars: He gives names to all of them.

Psalm 147:4 NAS

And there is no creature hidden from His sight, but all things are open and laid bare to the eyes of Him with whom we have to do.

Hebrews 4:13 NAS

O Lord, You have searched me and known me. You know when I sit down and when I rise up: You understand my thought from afar. You scrutinize my path and my lying down, and are intimately acquainted with all my ways. Even before there is a word on my tongue, Behold, O Lord, You know it all.

Psalm 139:1–4 NAS

Remember the former things long past, for I am God, and there is no other: I am God, and there is no one like Me, declaring the end from the beginning, and from ancient times things which have not been done, Saying, "My purpose will be established, and I will accomplish all My good pleasure."

Isaiah 46:9–10

Do you not know? Have you not heard? The Everlasting God, the Lord, the Creator of the ends of the earth does not become weary or tired, His understanding is inscrutable.

Isaiah 40:28 NAS

Then hear in heaven Your dwelling place, and forgive and act and render to each according to all his ways, whose heart You know, for You alone know the hearts of all the sons of men.

1 Kings 8:39 NAS

And they prayed and said, "You, Lord, who know the hearts of all men, show which one of these two You have chosen.

Acts 1:24 NAS

Jesus said in Matthew 16 that when we think like men, we become our own stumbling block. What we think and how we think are very important. Wrong thinking inevitably trips us up. We need to get rid of our old way of thinking like mere men and have a fresh way of thinking. We need to think like God.

Jesus turned and said to Peter, "Get behind me, Satan! You are a stumbling block to me; you do not have in mind the concerns of God, but merely human concerns."

Matthew 16:23 NIV

You may ask, "Is it even possible to think like God?" To answer a question like this, we need to first understand that when God makes a statement, He does so from the premise of knowing that not only is it *possible* for us to think like He does, but, more importantly, He *wants* us to think like He does.

God's eternal plan started long before He created anything or anyone, and this plan includes His desire for us to have His thoughts and to think like He thinks.

His Will

Having made known unto us the Mystery of His will, according to His good pleasure which He hath purposed in Himself.

Ephesians 1:9 KJV

His Plan

How blessed is God! And what a blessing He is! He's the Father of our Master, Jesus Christ, and takes us to the high places of blessing in him. Long before he laid down earth's foundations, He had us in mind, had settled on us as the focus of His love, to be made whole and holy by His love. Long, long ago He decided to adopt us into His family through Jesus Christ. (What pleasure He took in planning this!) He wanted us to enter into the celebration of His lavish gift-giving by the hand of His beloved Son.

Ephesians 1:3–6 The Message

His Motivation

God the Father, God the Son, and God the Holy Spirit (the Godhead) had a meeting way before creation, and they decided that their desire was to create us for the purpose of adoption into the family of God through our Lord Jesus Christ. Not only did He decide to create us, but we were what inspired Him to create in the first place. All He ever wanted was for us to experience His life—the reason He created us.

Redeemed to Participate in His Lifestyle

He also redeemed us for the purpose of participating in His life.

In whom we have redemption through His blood, the forgiveness of sins, according to the riches of His grace.
Ephesians 1:7

Invited to Participate in His Lifestyle

Not only did He redeem us to participate in His lifestyle, but He also desires and invites us to participate in it.

The eyes of your understanding being enlightened: that ye may know what is the hope of His calling, and what the riches of the glory of His inheritance in the saints.

Ephesians 1:18

CHAPTER 1

The Life of God

What Is the Life of God?

As we consider the life of our Lord Jesus Christ, we find that God's life is first other-oriented.

And lo a voice from heaven, saying, this is My beloved Son, in whom I am well pleased.

Matthew 3:17

The Father Exalts the Son

In Matthew 17, we see that the Father interrupted Peter, who had just spoken about making three tabernacles—that is, one for the Lord, one for Moses, and one for Elijah. We have Moses, who represents the law, and Elijah, who represents the prophets, but God the Father makes the distinction among the Lord Jesus, the law, and the prophets by saying, "This is My beloved Son in whom I am well pleased: hear ye Him." Although it is clear that God the Father wants you to hear the Lord Jesus, today we hear a lot of people following Moses and Elijah and listening more to the law and the prophets than to the Lord Jesus Himself. Let us follow the desire of our Father in heaven and listen first and foremost to his beloved Son, the Lord Jesus Christ.

While He yet spake, behold, a bright cloud overshadowed them: and behold a voice out of the cloud, which said, This is My beloved Son, in whom I am well pleased: hear ye Him.

Matthew 17:5

The Lord Jesus Exalts the Father

My Father, which gave them me, is greater than all: and no man is able to pluck them out of My Father's hand.

John 10:29

For I have not spoken of Myself: but the Father which sent Me, He gave Me a commandment, what I should say, and what I should speak.

John 12:49

The Lord Jesus Exalts the Holy Spirit

Nevertheless I tell you the truth: It is expedient for you that I go away: for if I go not away, the Comforter will not come unto you: but if I depart, I will send him unto you.

John 16:7

The Holy Spirit Exalts the Lord Jesus

We can clearly see through the scriptures that the first characteristic of the life of God is to be other-oriented.

> *He shall glorify me: for he shall receive of mine, and shall shew it unto you.*
>
> John 16:14

The Lord Jesus is the perfect representation of our Father God. If there was anyone on earth that lived His life for others, that person was our Lord Jesus. He lived to save, raise from the dead, heal, deliver, feed, bless, comfort, and serve all people who came in touch with Him and who were willing to receive from Him. He never got married or built a career for Himself, but He lived and died for us. He is the perfect picture of God for us.

> *He hath in these last days spoken unto us by His Son, whom He hath appointed heir of all things, by whom also He made the worlds: Who being the brightness of His glory, and the express image of His person, and upholding all things by the word of His power, when He had by Himself purged our sins, sat down on the right hand of the Majesty on high.*
>
> Hebrews 1:2–3

He even gave us the secret of happiness, which is participating in His life.

> *If ye know these things, happy are ye if ye do them.*
>
> John 13:17

The whole context is being other-oriented and serving others; therefore, happiness in life is to be other-oriented and to serve others with no strings attached, regardless of what we do.

SELF-SACRIFICIAL LIFE OF GOD

The life of God is not just an other-oriented life, but it is a life of unconditional love and acceptance, a self-sacrificial life, as well as a life marked by everything being done from a willing heart.

The self-sacrificial life is apparent in the following passages from the book of Revelation. The apostle John took a symbol of power, the lion, and turned it on its head, showing us in verse 6 that the lion is a lamb, as it has been slain. The power of God is in the self-sacrificial power of the lamb. God Almighty, who could have used His power to cause people to follow Him, chose the way of love and sacrifice to conquer the world because that is the greatest power that ever existed. God is love (1 John 4:8).

> *And one of the elders saith unto me, Weep not: behold, the Lion of the tribe of Judah, the Root of David, hath prevailed to open the book, and to lose the seven seals thereof. And I beheld, and, lo, in the midst of the throne and of the four beasts, and in the midst of the elders, stood a Lamb as it had been slain, having seven horns and seven eyes, which are the seven Spirits of God sent forth into all the earth.*
> Revelation 5:5–6

> *They follow the Lamb wherever He goes.*
> Revelation 14:4 NAS

In the following passage, the Warrior with eyes as a flame of fire, His vesture dipped in blood, and a sharp sword coming out of His mouth, followed by an army clothed in fine linen, white and clean, shows us that He is not coming *from* battle but going *to* battle. His clothing, which is dipped in blood, is dipped in *His own* blood, and the sword is the truth about His self-sacrificial love with which He does war against the lies that the nations believed. Those same nations are the nations over which He rules. The power of God is the self-sacrificial love on display for us through the sacrifice of our Lord Jesus Christ.

> *And I saw Heaven opened, and behold a white horse: and He that sat upon him was called Faithful and True, and in righteousness He doth judge and make war. His eyes were as a flame of fire, and on His head were many crowns: and He had a name written, that no man knew, but He Himself. And He was clothed with a vesture dipped in blood: and His name is called The Word of God. And the armies which were in Heaven followed Him upon white horses, clothed in fine linen, white and clean. And out of His mouth goeth a sharp sword, that with it He should smite the nations: and He shall rule them with a rod of iron: and He treadeth the winepress of the fierceness and wrath of Almighty God. And He hath on His vesture and on His thigh a name written, KING OF KINGS AND LORD OF LORDS.*
>
> Revelation 19:11–16

THINK LIKE GOD

Why is it so important to think like God does? Thinking like God will result in living like God, and living like God will result in being able to do what God does. Just as you think in your heart, so are you.

> *For as he thinketh in his heart, so is he: Eat and drink, saith he to thee: but his heart is not with thee.*
>
> Proverbs 23:7

Imagine being able to think like God. Wouldn't that be the most important thing you could do in your life?

> *For My thoughts are not your thoughts, neither are your ways My ways, saith the LORD. For as the heavens are higher than the earth, so are My ways higher than your ways, and My thoughts than your thoughts.*
>
> Isaiah 55:8–9

CHAPTER 2

Repentance and Receiving from God

The Bible talks about the renewing of our minds, called repentance. In the Old Testament, the word *repentance* meant to be sorry, cry, dress in sackcloth and put ashes on your head, fast and pray, etc. However, in the New Testament, under the new covenant, the word *repentance* takes on a whole new meaning; it means to change the way you think, to be transformed by the renewing of your mind.

In Romans, we read,

> *I beseech you therefore, brethren, by the mercies of God, that ye present your bodies a living sacrifice, holy, acceptable unto God, which is your reasonable service. And be not conformed to this world: but be ye transformed by the renewing of your mind, that ye may prove what is that good, and acceptable, and perfect, will of God.*
>
> Romans 12:1–2

The key phrase in the first verse of Romans 12 is "present your bodies a living sacrifice." In order to present our bodies, those bodies must have already been made a living sacrifice, holy and acceptable unto God by the Lord Jesus when He died on the cross. This is evidenced by the fact that we died together with Christ and that we were raised together with Him to be seated with Him in heavenly places.

> *For the love of Christ constraineth us: because we thus judge, that if one died for all, then were all dead.*
> 2 Corinthians 5:14

> *But God, who is rich in mercy, for His great love wherewith He loved us, Even when we were dead in sins, hath quickened us together with Christ, (by grace ye are saved:) And hath raised us up together, and made us sit together in heavenly places in Christ Jesus.*
> Ephesians 2:4–6

Like I said, to present my body as a living sacrifice first means that my body was already made a living sacrifice, and I just need to present it. For example, if I present to you a Bible, it would mean that the Bible already exists. I'm not making the Bible; I'm simply presenting it to you.

In the second verse of Romans 12, the key phrase is "transformed by the renewing of your mind." If the renewing of our minds was not possible, the apostle Paul would not have made this statement. The Lord Jesus said,

> *And saying, the time is fulfilled, and the kingdom of God is at hand: repent ye, and believe the gospel.*
> Matthew 1:15

In other words, change the way you think, and believe the good news that salvation is not by what you do, but is a free gift through our Lord Jesus Christ, for this is the mind-set of the kingdom of God. This way of thinking is diametrically opposed to what religion has taught us. We need to allow the Word of God to change the way we think so we can benefit from all that the kingdom of God has to offer.

RECEIVING AS A LITTLE CHILD IS THE MINDSET OF HEAVEN

> *Verily I say unto you, whosoever shall not receive the kingdom of God as a little child, he shall not enter therein.*
>
> Mark 10:15

If we are going to receive as a little child, it behooves us to learn how a little child receives. There are several characteristics required in order for a child to receive. Those characteristics are that they must be:

Simple

> *But God chose the foolish things of the world to shame the wise: God chose the weak things of the world to shame the strong.*
>
> 1 Corinthians 1:27

Easy

> *Come unto Me, all ye that labour and are heavy laden, and I will give you rest. Take My yoke upon you, and*

> *learn of Me: for I am meek and lowly in heart: and ye*
> *shall find rest unto your souls. For My yoke is easy, and*
> *My burden is light.*
>
> Matthew 11:28–30

Free

> *He that spared not his own Son, but delivered him up*
> *for us all, how shall he not with him also freely give us*
> *all things?*
>
> Romans 8:32

> *Heal the sick, raise the dead, cleanse those who have*
> *leprosy, drive out demons. Freely you have received:*
> *freely give.*
>
> Matthew 10:8

Immediate

> *(For he saith, I have heard thee in a time accepted, and*
> *in the day of salvation have I succoured thee: behold,*
> *now is the accepted time: behold, now is the day of*
> *salvation).*
>
> 2 Corinthians 6:2

When I tell my seven-year-old daughter, Harmony, that I will take her to the park, here is what she is *not* thinking:

> ➤ It's too complicated to go to the park. (**It's simple.**)
> ➤ Going to the park takes too much effort. (**It's easy.**)
> ➤ I have to work to pay for this. I'm not worthy to go to the park. (**It's free.**)

> ➤ It's going to be later or someday in the future. She assumes it's now and already has her shoes on, waiting at the door for me to take her.

Why do so many believers not experience the kingdom? Because they don't expect receiving to be simple, easy, free, and immediate. All we need to do is allow our lives to be transformed by the renewing of our minds, according to the mentality of heaven.

CHAPTER 3

Humans and Their Value

Jesus said that the value of a human soul can't be measured. If we were to add all the money from all the banks in the world—all currency, all platinum, gold, silver, diamonds, cars, real estate, oil, water, mountains, the stars, the moon, the sun, all galaxies, and all that God created—it would not even come close to the value of one human soul.

> *For what shall it profit a man, if he shall gain the whole world, and lose his own soul?*
>
> Mark 8:36

Why do we have such great value in the eyes of God?

Because we were created in His image and His likeness.

> *Then God said, "Let Us make mankind in our image, in our likeness, so that they may rule over the fish in the sea and the birds in the sky, over the livestock and all the wild animals, and over all the creatures that move along the ground."*
>
> Genesis 1:26

We have the image and the superscription of God on us, and that's what makes us valuable.

> *Show Me a penny. Whose image and superscription hath it? They answered and said, Caesar's. And He said unto them, Render therefore unto Caesar the things which be Caesar's, and unto God the things which be God's.*
>
> Luke 20:24–25

Because we are created by God. Just as the value of artwork is based on the artist who created it, we are valuable because of Him who created us, God Himself, the Creator.

> *For we are His workmanship, created in Christ Jesus unto good works, which God hath before ordained that we should walk in them.*
>
> Ephesians 2:10

Because of the price that was paid for us.

> *Forasmuch as ye know that ye were not redeemed with corruptible things, as silver and gold, from your vain conversation received by tradition from your fathers: But with the precious blood of Christ, as of a lamb without blemish and without spot.*
>
> 1 Peter 1:18–19

There are three parables our Lord gives in Luke 15 to answer people who were judging Him for hanging out with sinners and tax collectors, who were considered the worst sinners because they worked for the Roman Empire to collect taxes from the people of Israel.

1. The parable of the lost sheep shows us that a lost sheep has the same value to the shepherd as the one that's not lost.
2. The parable of the lost coin shows us that even if the coin was lost, dirty, or in a dark place, it still has the same value as the nine that were not lost.
3. The parable of the prodigal son shows us that the son who was lost had the same value as the one who stayed with his father.

Our value does not depend on our merits, level of intelligence, skin color, checkbook, nationality, social status, or anything else but God Himself. That's the reason our Lord Jesus said:

> *And the King shall answer and say unto them, Verily I say unto you, Inasmuch as ye have done it unto one of the least of these My brethren, ye have done it unto Me.*
>
> Matthew 25:40

Furthermore, in Matthew, the Lord shared two other parables about the hidden treasure and the pearl.

> *The kingdom of heaven is like a treasure hidden in a field. One day a man found the treasure, and then he hid it in the field again. The man was very happy to find the treasure. He went and sold everything that he owned to buy that field. Also, the kingdom of heaven is like a man looking for fine pearls. One day he found a very valuable pearl. The man went and sold everything he had to buy that pearl.*
>
> Matthew 13:44–46

Notice that in these parables, the hidden treasure and the pearl represent us, and God is the one selling everything He has just to have us. Also, realize that we were the treasure before He found us, and we were the pearl of great value before He found us.

Let's treat all people with dignity, honor, and value, as the Lord would.

CHAPTER 4

God's Justice/Righteousness v. Human Justice

The word for *justice* in the Hebrew language is *tsadeq* or *tsadoq,* which means "to be right or righteous, acquit, acquitted, declare you right, do justice, give him justice, properly restored, proved right, vindicated, vindicates" (Strong's Concordance, 6663).

In studying God's justice, I found it very interesting that nowhere in the definition did I find *punishment* or *condemnation.* God's justice is always restorative and never punitive. Let's look at a few passages from scripture where the word *justice* appears. According to the following passage of scripture, the Sun of Righteousness (justice) arises with healing in His wings. Justice is equated to healing.

> But unto you that fear My name shall the Sun of
> righteousness arise with healing in His wings: and ye
> shall go forth, and grow up as calves of the stall.
> Malachi 4:2

In the following verse from Romans, we see that the righteousness or justice of God is revealed in the gospel, meaning this is not condemning or punishing but rather restorative and uplifting:

> *For I am not ashamed of the gospel of Christ: for it is the power of God unto salvation to everyone that believeth: to the Jew first, and also to the Greek. For therein is the righteousness of God revealed from faith to faith: as it is written, the just shall live by faith.*
>
> Romans 1:16–17

God also tells us to be on the side of the oppressed, the fatherless, and the widow. In other words, help the ones in need. This looks to me more like mercy, and that's because in God's mind, mercy and justice are not opposites, but twins, coming from the same womb of compassion.

> *Learn to do well: seek judgment, relieve the oppressed, judge the fatherless, plead for the widow.*
>
> Isaiah 1:17

We also discover that when God judges, He judges to have mercy on people and to be gracious unto them:

> *And therefore will the Lord wait, that He may be gracious unto you, and therefore will He be exalted, that He may have mercy upon you: for the Lord is a God of judgment: blessed are all they that wait for Him.*
>
> Isaiah 30:18

According to God, executing true justice requires showing mercy and compassion to all.

> *Thus speaketh the Lord of hosts, saying, execute true judgment, and shew mercy and compassions every man to his brother.*
>
> Zechariah 7:9

Regarding Ephraim, God does not enter the city to destroy it, because He is God and not a man, and He's full of compassion and mercy.

> *I will not execute the fierceness of mine anger, I will not return to destroy Ephraim: for I am God, and not man: the Holy One in the midst of thee: and I will not enter into the city.*
>
> Hosea 11:9

We see in the following verse that the Lord is judging the Gentiles. The real question is, how does He judge? Again we can see that He judges to have mercy. He says that a bruised reed He will not break and a smoking flax He will not quench. I don't know about you, but I like this kind of judgment. This is what causes the Gentiles to trust Him.

> *Behold My servant, whom I have chosen: My beloved, in whom My soul is well pleased: I will put My spirit upon Him, and He shall shew judgment to the Gentiles. He shall not strive, nor cry: neither shall any man hear His voice in the streets. A bruised reed shall He not break, and smoking flax shall He not quench, till He send forth judgment unto victory. And in His name shall the Gentiles trust.*
>
> Matthew 12:18–21

God's justice is done every time the gospel is preached to the poor; the brokenhearted are healed; the captives are set free; the blind recover their sight; the ones who are bruised are set at liberty; and the acceptable year of the Lord is preached.

> *The Spirit of the Lord is upon Me, because He hath anointed Me to preach the gospel to the poor: He hath sent Me to heal the brokenhearted, to preach deliverance to the captives, and recovering of sight to the blind, to set at liberty them that are bruised, To preach the acceptable year of the Lord.*
>
> Luke 4:18–19

In other words, God's justice is served every time sinners are forgiven, the sick are healed, the captives are set free, the blind see, the poor are made rich, and the dead are raised—and all this is without any payment on our part.

DEATH IS AN ENEMY TO BE DESTROYED AND NOT A REQUIREMENT OF JUSTICE

> *For He must reign, till He hath put all enemies under His feet. The last enemy that shall be destroyed is death.*
>
> 1 Corinthians 15:25–26

If the justice of God was satisfied at the cross through death, then the resurrection of Jesus would have been the undoing of it all; however, if death is the wages of sin and not justice, then the resurrection of our Lord is the declaration of God that justice was done through the resurrection.

> *So when this corruptible shall have put on incorruption,
> and this mortal shall have put on immortality, then
> shall be brought to pass the saying that is written,
> Death is swallowed up in victory. O death, where is thy
> sting? O grave, where is thy victory? The sting of death
> is sin: and the strength of sin is the law. But thanks be
> to God, which giveth us the victory through our Lord
> Jesus Christ.*
>
> 1 Corinthians 15:54–57

On the surface, it appears that God took pleasure in punishing Jesus for our sin.

> *Yet it pleased the LORD to bruise Him: He hath put
> Him to grief: when Thou shalt make His soul an
> offering for sin, He shall see His seed, He shall prolong
> His days, and the pleasure of the LORD shall prosper
> in His hand.*
>
> Isaiah 53:10

However, let us see how this is translated in the Brenton Septuagint, which is one of the most trusted translations of the Bible:

> *The Lord also is pleased to purge Him from His stroke.
> If ye can give an offering for sin, your soul shall see a
> long-lived seed.*
>
> Isaiah 53:10

As we see in this translation, the Lord is pleased to heal the Lord Jesus from "His stroke," meaning God was pleased to heal and resurrect the Lord Jesus from the dead. Here is a simple example of what I'm saying: Let's say my daughter, Harmony, acts disobediently, and my son gets in the middle. If I killed my son for

Harmony's disobedience, everything would be well between my daughter, who disobeyed me, and me because I would have calmed down and had my payment. What then would you think about me? Would not the authorities put me in prison? And rightfully so. Why is it that people say that about God?

On the other hand, I have two options: either forgive Harmony or punish her. One thing I do know is that I can't have both, because they do not go hand in hand, as they are opposites.

The definition of *righteousness* or *justice* in the Greek is *dicaisune* (Strong's Concordance 1343): "justness, righteousness, righteousness of which God is the source, divine righteousness, judicial approval, properly restored." Thayer's Greek Lexicon puts it this way: "the state of him who is as he ought to be."

God's justice is very different from human justice. We think justice is served when someone is placed in jail. God, on the other hand, thinks justice is served when people are released. Human justice says if one kills someone, justice is served when the criminal is sentenced to prison. However, God's justice is served when the one who was killed is raised from the dead, completely healed of all trauma sustained, and the criminal is restored, as are all affected by the act. God wants restoration not punishment. Try to see things from God's perspective.

God is the rightful owner of everyone and everything, so it would not be just for Him to pay to have us back. But He did it out of love. If someone kidnapped a child, it would not be just for the parents to pay to have the child back. They should receive the child back without having to pay anything, but I'm sure that, out of love, any parent would gladly do it.

> *The earth is the L*ORD*'s, and the fullness thereof:*
> *the world, and they that dwell therein. For he hath*
> *founded it upon the seas, and established it upon the*
> *floods.*
>
> Psalm 24:1–2

As we can see from the following verse, Jesus did not suffer for God, and it was not the chastisement of God's peace upon Him, but ours. Our Lord died for us, not for God.

> *Surely He hath borne our griefs, and carried our*
> *sorrows: yet we did esteem Him stricken, smitten*
> *of God, and afflicted. But He was wounded for our*
> *transgressions, He was bruised for our iniquities: the*
> *chastisement of our peace was upon Him: and with*
> *His stripes we are healed.*
>
> Isaiah 53:4–5

We were alienated and enemies of God in our own minds; therefore, a price had to be paid so our conscience would be purified through the blood of our Lord Jesus.

> *And you, that were sometime alienated and enemies*
> *in your mind by wicked works, yet now hath He*
> *reconciled in the body of His flesh through death, to*
> *present you holy and unblameable and unreproveable*
> *in His sight.*
>
> Colossians 1:21–22

The truth is that a payment was made; however, it was not made to the devil (the devil is a thief), because he does not deserve a payment. The payment was not made to God, because God did not demand a payment. The payment was made to our conscience, or else we would not have come back to God. This is important to know because this revelation about the fact that God's justice does not require a payment sets people free to forgive others freely, just as God forgave us. God has forgiven us, not because He got His payment, but simply because He is a forgiving God. Forgiveness is part of His nature.

> *How much more shall the blood of Christ, who through the eternal Spirit offered Himself without spot to God, purge your conscience from dead works to serve the living God?*
>
> Hebrews 9:14

> *For the law having a shadow of good things to come, and not the very image of the things, can never with those sacrifices which they offered year by year continually make the comers thereunto perfect. For then would they not have ceased to be offered? because that the worshippers once purged should have had no more conscience of sins.*
>
> Hebrews 10:1–2

The human idea of justice is presented so much in church today, and then we turn around and ask people to forgive freely, unconditionally, eternally, and completely—in other words, to operate according to God's justice. But it goes directly against what they've heard and have been taught. The two systems do not work together. God's justice says you do not need a payment. No one needs to apologize to you before you can forgive; you can do it freely.

Knowing that God's Spirit and God's nature are in us frees us to forgive everyone unconditionally. I love how The Message paraphrase of the Bible expresses this truth about forgiveness:

> *If you forgive someone's sins, they're gone for good. If*
> *you don't forgive sins, what are you going to do with*
> *them?*
>
> John 20:23

Some people carry unforgiveness in their hearts for twenty, thirty, forty years. They allow the same act to torture them for years instead of forgiving (sending away all judgments and feelings from their heart) just as God did once and for all.

The apostle Peter stated it this way:

> *Therefore let all Israel be assured of this: God has*
> *made this Jesus, whom you crucified, both Lord and*
> *Messiah.*
>
> Acts 2:36 NIV

Our Lord Jesus dying on the cross was not the punishment of God, for if justice was had in the death of Jesus, the resurrection would have countered all that was done in His death. Humankind crucified our Lord. We poured our treachery and sin on Him. We used violence against Him, and He took it all and died with it. If we say God punished Jesus, we make God a violent God, and we say violence is good.

The justice of God is revealed in the resurrection of Jesus: God declared His justice by raising Jesus from the dead. The justice of God is served every time someone experiences forgiveness, freedom, healing, prosperity, life, comfort, unconditional acceptance, and love.

CHAPTER 5

The Vengeance of God

When we think about vengeance, we think of something frightening and someone taking revenge on someone else. I remember talking to the Lord one time about the following passage:

> *Dearly beloved, avenge not yourselves, but rather give place unto wrath: for it is written, Vengeance is mine: I will repay, saith the Lord. Therefore if thine enemy hunger, feed him: if he thirst, give him drink: for in so doing thou shalt heap coals of fire on his head. Be not overcome of evil, but overcome evil with good.*
>
> Romans 12:19–21

I asked the Lord, "How come You can take revenge but You would not allow me to take revenge?"

He answered, "Because your revenge is not My kind of revenge."

Again, I stated, "Oh, I see. You want me to do something good to someone who did evil to me to prove me right and them wrong."

He answered, "Son, I'm not interested in endorsing your ego. Where else in the Bible do you find anything written about hot coals?"

I answered, "Isaiah 6:5–7," which says,

> *Then said I, Woe is me! for I am undone: because I am a man of unclean lips, and I dwell in the midst of a people of unclean lips: for mine eyes have seen the King, the LORD of hosts. Then flew one of the seraphims unto me, having a live coal in his hand, which he had taken with the tongs from off the altar: And he laid it upon MY mouth, and said, Lo, this hath touched thy lips: and thine iniquity is taken away, and thy sin purged.*
>
> Isaiah 6:5–7

The Lord answered, "You see, placing hot coals on someone removes that person's iniquity, so likewise, when you respond with good to an evil done against you, you remove the evil influence from that person's life so they are free to make the right choices."

GOD'S VENGEANCE IS NOT AGAINST HUMAN BEINGS, BUT AGAINST EVIL

According to the following scripture, the vengeance of God is to comfort all that mourn, to give beauty for ashes, the oil of joy for mourning, and the garment of praise for the spirit of heaviness. That's how God is glorified.

> *The Spirit of the Lord God is upon me: because the Lord hath anointed me to preach good tidings unto the meek: he hath sent me to bind up the brokenhearted,*

to proclaim liberty to the captives, and the opening of the prison to them that are bound: To proclaim the acceptable year of the Lord, and the day of vengeance of our God: to comfort all that mourn: To appoint unto them that mourn in Zion, to give unto them beauty for ashes, the oil of joy for mourning, the garment of praise for the spirit of heaviness: that they might be called trees of righteousness, the planting of the Lord, that he might be glorified.

Isaiah 61:1–3

The best definition of God's vengeance that I can use is that God puts His goodness on steroids to reach us. I don't know about you, but this makes me shout "LORD, I WANT MORE OF YOUR VENGEANCE!"

CHAPTER 6

Faith in God

We need to know that faith is not what we produce, but rather our response to hearing the gospel, the good news about the finished work of the cross through the unconditional love of God and all that God has accomplished for all people of all times because of His love, grace, faithfulness, goodness, etc. In order for authentic faith to arise within us, we need to have knowledge of a few things.

First, we need to know that God is omniscient and that He knows all things. In the introduction to this book, I listed a lot of scriptures revealing the omniscience of God.

Next, we need to know that God is almighty and that He can do all things.

> *Yours, Lord, is the greatness and the power and the glory and the majesty and the splendor, for everything in heaven and earth is yours. Yours, Lord, is the kingdom: you are exalted as head over all. Both riches and honour come of thee, and thou reignest*

over all: and in thine hand is power and might: and in thine hand it is to make great, and to give strength unto all.

1 Chronicles 29:11–12

Ah, Lord God! Behold, You have made the heavens and the earth by Your great power and outstretched arm. There is nothing too hard for You.

Jeremiah 32:17

Next, we need to know that God is deeply, irreversibly, irrevocably, and unconditionally in love with us.

But God commendeth his love toward us, in that, while we were yet sinners, Christ died for us.

Romans 5:8

Who shall separate us from the love of Christ? shall tribulation, or distress, or persecution, or famine, or nakedness, or peril, or sword?

Romans 8:35

Ye have heard that it hath been said, Thou shalt love thy neighbour, and hate thine enemy. But I say unto you, Love your enemies, bless them that curse you, do good to them that hate you, and pray for them which despitefully use you, and persecute you: That ye may be the children of your Father which is in heaven: for he maketh his sun to rise on the evil and on the good, and sendeth rain on the just and on the unjust. For if ye love them which love you, what reward have ye? do not even the publicans the same? And if ye salute your brethren only, what do ye more

> *than others? do not even the publicans so? Be ye therefore*
> *perfect, even as your Father which is in heaven is perfect.*
> Matthew 5:43–48

Let's start at the end of the above chapter, in verse 48, which we know is the conclusion. Most people read this verse and think this is just what God wants from us without seeing that our Lord Jesus is presenting to us the true nature of God Himself in saying, "Even as your Father which is in heaven is perfect."

Based on this, we can surely state the following:

➢ God loves His enemies;
➢ God blesses those who curse Him;
➢ God does good to them that hate Him;
➢ God prays for those who despitefully use Him and persecute Him;
➢ God makes His sun to rise on the evil and on the good; and
➢ God sends rain on the just and the unjust.

We can see this in the life and the death of our Lord Jesus, who said, "Father, forgive them, for they do not know what they are doing" (Luke 23:34). The good news is that this God lives in you if you have accepted Him as your Lord and Savior, and this is the only life that He knows to live and the only love He displays.

Next, we need to know that God is good towards us all the time and that His goodness is independent of our actions. God's thoughts toward you are of peace and not of evil. The idea that God is giving you something bad to teach you something contradicts this scripture.

> *For I know the thoughts that I think toward you, saith the* LORD, *thoughts of peace, and not of evil, to give you an expected end.*
>
> Jeremiah 29:11

James said it this way:

> *Every good gift and every perfect gift is from above, and cometh down from the Father of lights, with whom is no variableness, neither shadow of turning.*
>
> James 1:17

If it's not good, not of peace, not a gift, or not perfect, then it's not from God.

Next, we need to know that God is faithful to us even when we are not faithful to Him.

> *If we are faithless, He remains faithful: He cannot deny Himself.*
>
> 2 Timothy 2:13 NKJV

These are all key ingredients needed for the birth of authentic faith through a relationship with God, a faith that can't be shaken.

CHAPTER 7

Sin and Condemnation

___

The definition of sin is to miss the mark by not participating in the life of God.

> *For the wages of sin is death, but the gift of God is*
> *eternal life in Christ Jesus our Lord.*
>
> Romans 6:23

God is the source of all life, goodness, love, blessing, and every good and perfect gift. To depart from the Generator of life would mean death.

It's true that the Lamb of God took away any excuse we may have to stay away from God. He did this by showing the greatest display of love this world has ever seen or ever will see: He died for all of us on the cross. He loved us so much that He said, "I'd rather die than be without them." And then not even death could hold Him, for His love for us is way greater than death.

*The next day John saw Jesus coming toward him and
said, "Look, the Lamb of God, who takes away the sin
of the world!"*

John 1:29 NIV

In the following verses, we see the one thing Jesus was *not* sent
to do: to condemn the world. Nevertheless, in many churches
today, a feeling of heaviness and condemnation is confused with
the presence of God. Nothing could be further from the truth.
Condemnation is not from God. You can line yourself up with one
of these two choices: condemnation or salvation. Since God is in
the business of salvation and not condemnation, the smart thing to
do is to align with God.

*There is therefore now no condemnation to them
which are in Christ Jesus, who walk not after the flesh,
but after the Spirit.*

Romans 8:1

*For God sent not his Son into the world to condemn
the world: but that the world through him might be
saved.*

John 3:17

As you can see from the next scriptures, all our sins have already
been forgiven according to the riches of His grace because of His
blood and for His name's sake.

*In whom we have redemption through his blood, the
forgiveness of sins, according to the riches of his grace.*

Ephesians 1:7

> *And you, being dead in your sins and the uncircumcision of your flesh, hath he quickened together with him, having forgiven you all trespasses.*
>
> Colossians 2:13

> *I write unto you, little children, because your sins are forgiven you for his name's sake.*
>
> 1 John 2:12

You might ask, *what about future sins?* Well, let's see:

> *Simon Peter said unto him, Lord, whither goest thou? Jesus answered him, Whither I go, thou canst not follow me now: but thou shalt follow me afterwards. Peter said unto him, Lord, why cannot I follow thee now? I will lay down My life for thy sake. Jesus answered him, Wilt thou lay down thy life for My sake? Verily, verily, I say unto thee, the cock shall not crow, till thou hast denied me thrice.*
>
> John 13:36–38

> *Let not your heart be troubled: ye believe in God, believe also in me. In My Father's house are many mansions: if it were not so, I would have told you. I go to prepare a place for you. And if I go and prepare a place for you, I will come again, and receive you unto Myself: that where I am, there ye may be also.*
>
> John 14:1–3

In the original language of the Bible, there are no chapters. This means that the Lord Jesus was still talking to Peter. He is saying that Peter would deny him three times, and then he adds, "Don't let your heart be troubled. I will show up in heaven and you'll have a destiny with me." In other words, the way the Lord dealt with Peter's sin was to speak about his eternal destiny with Him. In the above verses, we see the Lord forgiving Peter's future sin. Does that mean we can do whatever we want? Well, no!

> *What shall we say then? Shall we continue in sin, that grace may abound? God forbid. How shall we, that are dead to sin, live any longer therein?*
>
> Romans 6:1–2

Not knowing or forgetting that you have been cleansed of your sin will make you unfruitful and barren, and it will rob you of the potential you have in Christ Jesus our Lord. You can now rest, knowing that your sins are forgiven.

> *And beside this, giving all diligence, add to your faith virtue: and to virtue knowledge: And to knowledge temperance: and to temperance patience: and to patience Godliness: And to Godliness brotherly kindness: and to brotherly kindness charity. For if these things be in you, and abound, they make you that ye shall neither be barren nor unfruitful in the knowledge of our Lord Jesus Christ. But he that lacketh these things is blind, and cannot see afar off, and hath forgotten that he was purged from his old sins.*
>
> 2 Peter 1:5–9

Chapter 8

The Grace of God

There is much talk today about the grace of God. Some people are all for the grace of God, and some are against the grace of God. Let's look at what the grace of God is and all the benefits grace offers us, as well as the main reason some people are against the grace message.

First, grace is not just a teaching, a message, or something believers could be for or against. Grace is a person, and His name is Jesus.

> *For the law was given by Moses, but grace and truth came by Jesus Christ.*
>
> John 1:17

The grace of God can be summed up as

- the unmerited favor of God toward us;
- the empowerment of God in our lives to live and fulfill the purpose for which we are here on earth; and
- the divine influence upon the heart, reflecting in our lives the character and life of our Lord Jesus Christ.

Without grace, there would be no favor.

> *But Noah found grace in the eyes of the Lord.*
>
> Genesis 6:8

Without grace, there would be no sufficiency.

> *And he said unto me, My grace is sufficient for thee: for*
> *My strength is made perfect in weakness. Most gladly*
> *therefore will I rather glory in MY infirmities, that the*
> *power of Christ may rest upon me.*
>
> 2 Corinthians 12:9

Without grace, there would be no free justification.

> *Therefore by the deeds of the law there shall no flesh be*
> *justified in his sight: for by the law is the knowledge of*
> *sin. But now the righteousness of God without the law is*
> *manifested, being witnessed by the law and the prophets:*
> *Even the righteousness of God which is by faith of Jesus*
> *Christ unto all and upon all them that believe: for there*
> *is no difference: For all have sinned, and come short*
> *of the glory of God: Being justified freely by his grace*
> *through the redemption that is in Christ Jesus.*
>
> Romans 3:20–24

Without grace, there would be no truth, no glory, and no Son of God.

> *And the Word was made flesh, and dwelt among*
> *us, (and we beheld his glory, the glory as of the only*
> *begotten of the Father,) full of grace and truth.*
>
> John 1:14

Without grace, there would be no apostleship and no call to obedience.

> *Paul, a servant of Jesus Christ, called to be an apostle, separated unto the gospel of God, (which he had promised afore by his prophets in the holy scriptures,) concerning his Son Jesus Christ our Lord, which was made of the seed of David according to the flesh: And declared to be the Son of God with power, according to the spirit of holiness, by the resurrection from the dead: By whom we have received grace and apostleship, for obedience to the faith among all nations, for his name.*
> Romans 1:1–5

Without grace, there would be no power.

> *Now Stephen, a man full of God's grace and power, performed great wonders and signs among the people.*
> Acts 6:8

Without grace, there would be no gift and no receiving from Christ.

> *But unto every one of us is given grace according to the measure of the gift of Christ.*
> Ephesians 4:7

Without grace, there would be no establishing or strengthening of your heart.

> *Do not be carried away by diverse and strange teachings: for it is good for the heart to be established and strengthened by grace and not by foods [rules of*

*diet and ritualistic meals], which bring no benefit or
spiritual growth to those who observe them.*

Hebrews 13:9

Without grace, there would be no compassion, no favor, no drawing
to Christ, and no salvation.

*For it is by grace [God's remarkable compassion
and favor drawing you to Christ] that you have been
saved [actually delivered from judgment and given
eternal life] through faith. And this [salvation] is not
of yourselves [not through your own effort], but it is
the [undeserved, gracious] gift of God: not as a result
of [your] works [nor your attempts to keep the Law],
so that no one will [be able to] boast or take credit in
any way [for his salvation].*

Ephesians 2:8–9 AMP

Without grace, there would be no peace.

*Grace and peace [that special sense of spiritual well-
being] be multiplied to you in the [true, intimate]
knowledge of God and of Jesus our Lord.*

2 Peter 1:2 AMP

Without grace, there would be no confidence, no mercy, no help
in time of need, and no blessing coming at just the right moment.

*Therefore let us [with privilege] approach the throne of
grace [that is, the throne of God's gracious favor] with
confidence and without fear, so that we may receive
mercy [for our failures] and find [His amazing]*

> *grace to help in time of need [an appropriate blessing,*
> *coming just at the right moment].*
>
> Hebrew 4:16 AMP

Without grace, there would be no gift, no servanthood, no faithfulness, and no stewardship.

> *Just as each one of you has received a special gift [a*
> *spiritual talent, an ability graciously given by God],*
> *employ it in serving one another as [is appropriate for]*
> *good stewards of God's multi-faceted grace [faithfully*
> *using the diverse, varied gifts and abilities granted to*
> *Christians by God's unmerited favor].*
>
> 1 Peter 4:10 AMP

Without grace, there would be no humility.

> *But he giveth more grace. Wherefore he saith, God*
> *resisteth the proud, but giveth grace unto the humble.*
>
> James 4:6

Without grace, there would be no generosity.

> *But since you excel in everything—in faith, in speech,*
> *in knowledge, in complete earnestness and in the love*
> *we have kindled in you—see that you also excel in this*
> *grace of giving.*
>
> 2 Corinthians 8:7 NIV

Without grace, there would be no salvation shown to all people, no teaching to deny ungodliness and worldly lusts, no living soberly, righteously, and godly in this present world, and no hope for the glorious appearing of the great God and Savior Jesus Christ.

For the grace of God that bringeth salvation hath appeared to all men, teaching us that, denying ungodliness and worldly lusts, we should live soberly, righteously, and Godly, in this present world: Looking for that blessed hope, and the glorious appearing of the great God and our Savior Jesus Christ.

Titus 2:11–13

Without grace, there would be no freedom from sin.

For sin shall not have dominion over you: for ye are not under the law, but under grace.

Romans 6:14

Without grace, there would be no forgiveness of sin.

In whom we have redemption through his blood, the forgiveness of sins, according to the riches of his grace.

Ephesians 1:7

Without grace, there would be no love and no mercy.

But God, who is rich in mercy, for his great love wherewith he loved us, even when we were dead in sins, hath quickened us together with Christ, (by grace ye are saved:).

Ephesians 4:5

Without grace, there would be no ability to be slow to anger, no steadfast love, and no faithfulness.

But you, Lord, are a compassionate and gracious God, slow to anger, abounding in love and faithfulness.

Psalm 86:15

Without grace, there would be no identity, no existence in ministry, and no working more than all.

> *But by the grace of God I am what I am: and his grace which was bestowed upon me was not in vain: but I laboured more abundantly than they all: yet not I, but the grace of God which was with me.*
>
> 1 Corinthians 15:10

Is it *grace* or is it *works*? According this passage, grace works.

Without grace, there would be no peace with God, no faith, and no rejoicing in hope of the glory of God.

> *Therefore being justified by faith, we have peace with God through our Lord Jesus Christ: by whom also we have access by faith into this grace wherein we stand, and rejoice in hope of the glory of God.*
>
> Romans 5:1–2

Without grace, there would be no life.

> *Likewise, ye husbands, dwell with them according to knowledge, giving honour unto the wife, as unto the weaker vessel, and as being heirs together of the grace of life: that your prayers be not hindered.*
>
> 1 Peter 3:7

Without grace, there would be no gospel.

> *But none of these things move me, neither count I my life dear unto myself, so that I might finish my course*

*with joy, and the ministry, which I have received of the
Lord Jesus, to testify the gospel of the grace of God.*

Acts 20:24

Without grace, there would be no reigning, no righteousness, and
no eternal life.

*That as sin hath reigned unto death, even so might
grace reign through righteousness unto eternal life by
Jesus Christ our Lord.*

Romans 5:21

I believe that based upon all these scriptures, without the grace of
God, we can't enjoy anything.

Many people are against grace because they have seen people who
talk about the grace of God but not reflect the presence of God in
their own lives. Another prevalent comment about grace is that it is
a license to sin. I believe that the problem is not the grace message
but rather mixing the grace message with penal substitution. Penal
substitution basically states that God punished Jesus, and because
He punished our Lord Jesus, all of God's wrath was satisfied, so He
can't punish us any longer. Now, if anything gives people a license
to sin, this would have to be it. There are a few obvious problems
with this view of the atonement theory:

1. It creates a separation in the Trinity. We know that God
    was in Christ, reconciling the world to himself.

*To wit, that God was in Christ, reconciling the world
unto himself, not imputing their trespasses unto them:
and hath committed unto us the word of reconciliation.*

2 Corinthians 5:19

When the Lord Jesus prayed from the cross, He didn't say, "Father, I know why You punish Me." Rather, He cried out,

> *"Father, forgive them: for they know not what they do." And they parted his raiment, and cast lots.*
>
> Luke 23:34

2. It presents the Father God as being a blood-thirsty god looking for justice man's way, when all He ever wanted was to have His children back.
3. It makes the atonement all about human justice and not about relationship and love. God did not have a justice problem; rather, He had a communication and relationship problem—and that problem was not on his side but ours.
4. It creates the mind-set that if God required a payment, He would not forgive anyone until they apologized to Him. Penal substitution keeps people in the bondage of unforgiveness.

Mixing grace with penal substitution results in a lot of flaky Christians who do not care about God because they think, *God got His payment, and now He can't touch me because of Jesus.* Penal substitution mixed with grace is like mixing law and grace, and of course we all know that doesn't work.

If we understand that it was never about punishment but always was about love and relationship, the attitude of the believer changes to knowing just how greatly he or she is loved by the Divine.

CHAPTER 9

Rest According to God

To rest, according to the kingdom of this world, is to cease from all activity. We often say we need a vacation, or we need a vacation from a vacation. The truth is that we can be physically rested while our minds are racing a hundred miles an hour. Fear can grab our hearts and minds and can cause us to have panic attacks due to stress created by the fear and anxiety.

To rest, according to the kingdom of God, does not mean ceasing all your activities. To the contrary, it means to trust God no matter what circumstances you are going through. This requires a conscious effort and involves a lot of action on your part in defending your belief system.

In the following verses, rest for Israel meant entering the Promised Land. However, we know they still had enemies to conquer, they still had to fight, and they still had to work the land.

> *Harden not your hearts, as in the provocation, in*
> *the day of temptation in the wilderness: When your*
> *fathers tempted me, proved me, and saw My works*

> *forty years. Wherefore I was grieved with that*
> *generation, and said, they do alway err in their heart:*
> *and they have not known My ways. So I sware in My*
> *wrath, they shall not enter into My rest.*
>
> Hebrews 3:8–11

Rest in God's mind is receiving His promises by trusting Him.

What stopped the Israelites from entering the Promised Land (God's rest)? Their unbelief.

On the other hand, trusting God will manifest the following:

Peace

> *Be careful for nothing: but in everything by prayer and*
> *supplication with thanksgiving let your requests be*
> *made known unto God. And the peace of God, which*
> *passeth all understanding, shall keep your hearts and*
> *minds through Christ Jesus.*
>
> Philippians 4:6–7

The peace of God passes all understanding and keeps our minds and hearts through Christ Jesus, but verse 6 tells us to be careful for nothing but to pray and give thanks to God. We see that prayer is mostly for our minds and hearts to come into alignment with what is already true in the Spirit, and the result is the peace of God protecting us. This should not be hard, since the Lord Jesus has left us His peace.

> *Peace I leave with you, My peace I give unto you: not*
> *as the world giveth, give I unto you. Let not your heart*
> *be troubled, neither let it be afraid.*
>
> John 14:27

Our job is not to let our hearts be troubled, condemned, or afraid, and knowing that He lives in us makes this so simple. We just allow His life to flow through us, and peace is the result. The difference between worldly peace and God's peace is that the world has peace when there is no war and everything is perfect. With God's peace, we have peace in the midst of war and turmoil.

> *Thou preparest a table before me in the presence of mine enemies: thou anointest my head with oil: my cup runneth over.*
>
> Psalm 23:5

The Blessings of God

God has already blessed us with all spiritual blessings in Christ Jesus. Trusting God causes these blessings to manifest in our natural realm.

> *Blessed be the God and Father of our Lord Jesus Christ, who hath blessed us with all spiritual blessings in heavenly places in Christ.*
>
> Ephesians 1:3

All things pertaining to life and godliness have already been given to us by His divine power. All we need is to know Him and to trust Him.

> *According as his divine power hath given unto us all things that pertain unto life and Godliness, through the knowledge of him that hath called us to glory and virtue.*
>
> 2 Peter 1:3

The key word in the following verse is *freely.*

> *He that spared not his own Son, but delivered him up*
> *for us all, how shall he not with him also freely give us*
> *all things?*
>
> Romans 8:32

The reason so many people do not receive from God is because they want to obtain their inheritances from Him through their own efforts: they want to pay, and they work so hard to get it, but God says we can only have it for free.

Victory in Your Life

You can rest in God by giving thanks to the Lord for giving you the victory in Christ Jesus.

> *But thanks be to God, which giveth us the victory*
> *through our Lord Jesus Christ.*
>
> 1 Corinthians 15:57

The Lord Jesus has already overcome the world. This is good news because He lives in us and He gives us the victory, no matter what comes against us.

> *These things I have spoken unto you, that in me*
> *ye might have peace. In the world ye shall have*
> *tribulation: but be of good cheer: I have overcome the*
> *world.*
>
> John 16:33

The only condition to being a world overcomer through the faith we already have in Him is that you be born of God.

> *For whatsoever is born of God overcometh the world:*
> *and this is the victory that overcometh the world, even*
> *our faith.*
>
> 1 John 5:4

Knowing and believing that greater is He that is in us than He that is in the world should boost our confidence and give rest to our minds and hearts in Christ Jesus.

> *Ye are of God, little children, and have overcome them:*
> *because greater is he that is in you, than he that is in*
> *the world.*
>
> 1 John 4:4

You can rest in His provision of peace, blessing, and victory as He makes you to lie down in green pastures and leads you to still waters.

> *The Lord is my shepherd: I shall not want. He maketh*
> *me to lie down in green pastures: he leadeth me beside*
> *the still waters. He restoreth MY soul: he leadeth me*
> *in the paths of righteousness for his name's sake. Yea,*
> *though I walk through the valley of the shadow of*
> *death, I will fear no evil: for thou art with me: thy rod*
> *and thy staff they comfort me.*
>
> Psalm 23:1–4

In verse 3 of this wonderful psalm, the psalmist makes the following statements:

He Restores My Soul

This should bring rest to our hearts as we know that the responsibility to restore us is not ours but His. I am not against people receiving all kinds of help, but there are things only the Lord can fix. If this world had the answers to all the problems that exist today, we would be in much better shape than we are. However, we know that the world does not have the answers. Only God does.

He Leads Me in Paths of Righteousness (Restoration)

Not only has He restored our souls, but He leads us as well. Many people today allow their circumstances to lead them. Others allow prophets to lead them. I have nothing against prophets, but they should only confirm something that the Lord has already spoken to you.

Scripture says that we are to be led by the Spirit of God.

> *For as many as are led by the Spirit of God, they are the sons of God.*
>
> Romans 8:14

He Comforts Me

We are to allow the Comforter to comfort us. His name is the Holy Spirit.

> *But the Comforter, which is the Holy Ghost, whom the Father will send in my name, he shall teach you all things, and bring all things to your remembrance, whatsoever I have said unto you.*
>
> John 14:26

We can rest in His restoration, His leading, and His comfort. Again, *rest* in the kingdom of God is having peace in the midst of tribulation, knowing you already have the victory in Christ, and knowing that all His blessings already belong to you.

You can rest in God, knowing He restores your soul, He leads you, and He comforts you.

CHAPTER 10

The Mind of Christ

The Mind of Christ Is to Know the Things Freely Given to Us by God

This is a foreign concept to the system and mind-set of this world, which says nothing is free.

> Now we have received, not the spirit of the world, but the spirit which is of God: that we might know the things that are freely given to us of God. ... For who hath known the mind of the Lord, that he may instruct him? But we have the mind of Christ.
>
> 1 Corinthians 2:12, 16

The Spirit of God helps us to know intimately the things freely given to us by God, and that we have the mind of Christ.

The Mind of Christ Is to Humble Yourself and Serve

This concept is also foreign to this world. The word *servant* is viewed as a lowly position, and people have a hard time serving because of this. In the mind of Christ, humbling yourself and serving is the highest position you can obtain. Serving and humility are viewed as attributes of highest value in the kingdom of heaven and the family of God.

And James and John, the sons of Zebedee, come unto him, saying, Master, we would that thou shouldest do for us whatsoever we shall desire. And he said unto them, What would ye that I should do for you? They said unto him, Grant unto us that we may sit, one on thy right hand, and the other on thy left hand, in thy glory. But Jesus said unto them, Ye know not what ye ask: can ye drink of the cup that I drink of? and be baptized with the baptism that I am baptized with? And they said unto him, We can. And Jesus said unto them, Ye shall indeed drink of the cup that I drink of; and with the baptism that I am baptized withal shall ye be baptized: But to sit on my right hand and on my left hand is not mine to give; but it shall be given to them for whom it is prepared. And when the ten heard it, they began to be much displeased with James and John. But Jesus called them to him, and saith unto them, Ye know that they which are accounted to rule over the Gentiles exercise lordship over them; and their great ones exercise authority upon them. But so shall it not be among you: but whosoever will be great among you, shall be your minister: And whosoever of you will be the chiefest, shall be servant of all. For even the Son of man came not to be ministered unto, but to minister, and to give his life a ransom for many.

Mark 10:35–45

In the kingdom of heaven, the one who is in the highest position is the servant of all. The authority we have over each other is an authority to love and serve, not to dominate and manipulate people into a worldly submission.

As we look at Philippians 2 below, we see that the entire chapter deals with selfishness v. being other-oriented. In verses 3–5, we see that we need to allow the mind of Christ to be in us:

> *Let nothing be done through strife or vainglory; but in lowliness of mind let each esteem other better than themselves. Look not every man on his own things, but every man also on the things of others. Let this mind be in you, which was also in Christ Jesus.*

In verse 6, we see that the Lord Jesus Christ did not take advantage of people around Him because He is the Son of God:

> *Who, being in the form of God, thought it not robbery to be equal with God.*

In verse 7, we see that the Lord humbled Himself and served everyone around Him without expecting anything in return:

> *But made himself of no reputation, and took upon him the form of a servant, and was made in the likeness of men.*

In verse 8, we see that He accepted being a man and obeyed all the way up to the supreme sacrifice:

> *And being found in fashion as a man, he humbled himself, and became obedient unto death, even the death of the cross.*

For a long time, I believed that bowing before Jesus and confessing His lordship had to do with Him being almighty and forcing everyone to bow out of fear. However, looking at the word in Greek, I realized it is a reverential bow, and the context clearly states that when we realize what He's done and how He humbled Himself and served everyone, we gladly bow, not out of fear, but out of reverence before Him willingly.

> *Wherefore God also hath highly exalted him, and given him a name which is above every name: That at the name of Jesus every knee should bow, of things in heaven, and things in earth, and things under the earth; And that every tongue should confess that Jesus Christ is Lord, to the glory of God the Father.*
>
> Verses 9–11

As I look at the context of this book and chapter, I start understanding that the salvation the apostle Paul talks about here is a salvation from self and not from eternal damnation. We see this in verse 12:

> *Wherefore, my beloved, as ye have always obeyed, not as in my presence only, but now much more in my absence, work out your own salvation with fear and trembling.*

What I absolutely love about this is that God has the preeminent place in our hearts from where He gives us the will to work out our salvation from self and to become other-minded, which is the mind of Christ.

> *For it is God which worketh in you both to will and to do of his good pleasure.*
>
> Verse 13

> *Do all things without murmurings and disputings: That*
> *ye may be blameless and harmless, the sons of God,*
> *without rebuke, in the midst of a crooked and perverse*
> *nation, among whom ye shine as lights in the world.*
>
> Verses 14–15

The Mind of Christ Is for You to Submit to Be Loved and Served

In John 13, we see the Lord serving His disciples, and we can take note that the submission in this case is something Peter wasn't willing to accept in the beginning, as he said, "Thou shalt never wash my feet" (verse 8).

Later, we see Peter's submission to the love and serving of our Lord as he said to Him, "Lord, not my feet only, but also my hands and my head" (verse 9).

> *After that he poureth water into a basin, and began to*
> *wash the disciples' feet, and to wipe them with the towel*
> *wherewith he was girded. Then cometh he to Simon*
> *Peter: and Peter saith unto him, Lord, dost thou wash*
> *my feet? Jesus answered and said unto him, What I do*
> *thou knowest not now; but thou shalt know hereafter.*
> *Peter saith unto him, Thou shalt never wash my feet.*
> *Jesus answered him, If I wash thee not, thou hast no*
> *part with me. Simon Peter saith unto him, Lord, not*
> *my feet only, but also my hands and my head.*
>
> John 13:5–9

Submission in the kingdom of God is a submission to be loved and served, not to be dominated. It is a compound word, *sub mission*, but the mission should be one of love and service.

The best way I can say this would be that submission in the mind of God is the fruit of love received, or it is what one is willing to do when feeling loved and served genuinely.

The Mind of Christ Is for You to Be Free

With this in mind, let's look at a very familiar passage of scripture:

> *Out of respect for Christ, be courteously reverent to one another. Wives, understand and support your husbands in ways that show your support for Christ. The husband provides leadership to his wife the way Christ does to his church, not by domineering but by cherishing. So just as the church submits to Christ as he exercises such leadership, wives should likewise submit to their husbands. Husbands, go all out in your love for your wives, exactly as Christ did for the church—a love marked by giving, not getting. Christ's love makes the church whole. His words evoke her beauty. Everything he does and says is designed to bring the best out of her, dressing her in dazzling white silk, radiant with holiness. And that is how husbands ought to love their wives. They're really doing themselves a favor—since they're already "one" in marriage. No one abuses his own body, does he? No, he feeds and pampers it. That's how Christ treats us, the church, since we are part of his body. And this is why a man leaves father and mother and cherishes his wife. No longer two, they become "one flesh." This is a huge mystery, and I don't pretend to understand it all. What is clearest to me is the way Christ treats the church. And this provides a good picture of how each*

husband is to treat his wife, loving himself in loving her, and how each wife is to honor her husband.
Ephesians 5:21–33 The Message

As you can see, we are to submit to one another and wives are to submit to their husbands as unto the Lord. Why do we submit to the Lord in the first place? I don't know about you, but I submitted to Him because of His great love for me and because He gave His life for me.

If a wife is to submit to her husband as to the Lord, it must mean she needs to submit to her husband to be loved and served by him and not to be dominated by him. If this is not the case, we could say that God is an endorser of abuse, which cannot be.

Because of the world's mind-set regarding submission, which was incorporated into the church, so many times we find wives that stay in an abusive relationship, thinking they must because, after all, that's what Ephesians 5 speaks about. But that is simply not true.

You might ask, "Pastor John, you endorse divorce or separation?" No I do not, but I'm not going to endorse abuse either. I know this part of the book has the potential of making a lot of abusing husbands mad at me, but at the same time it has the potential of setting a lot of people free from being abused by husbands, controlling pastors, and other leaders within the church.

If you are in a relationship with a husband or church that abuses you, it's time for you to be free. Submit to love, submit to be served, and do not submit to abuse, for this is the will of God for you.

Oh, and by the way, doing dishes is not abuse. It's a necessity, and that goes for both husbands and wives.

CHAPTER 11

Union with God

This subject will get a lot of religious people mad at me, but at the same time it will set a lot of people who love God free from the bondage of religion and will allow them to fellowship with God 24/7, which is one of God's greatest desires.

God's declaration that He did not want to be God apart from humanity is obvious in the incarnation of our Lord Jesus Christ.

> *In the beginning was the Word, and the Word was with God, and the Word was God. And the Word was made flesh, and dwelt among us, (and we beheld his glory, the glory as of the only begotten of the Father,) full of grace and truth.*
>
> John 1:1, 14

The Lord Jesus, being born of God and the Virgin Mary, is forever going to be the perfect union between God and humankind, just as any of my children will forever be the union of my wife, Michaela, and myself. Just as you can't separate nor remove either myself or my wife from any of our children, as they are the result of our union, so it is with the union of God and humanity in our Lord Jesus Christ.

This gets better because He, the Lord Jesus, is the firstborn of many.

> *For whom he did foreknow, he also did predestinate to be conformed to the image of his Son, that he might be the firstborn among many brethren.*
>
> Romans 8:29

Just as the vine is one with the branch, so is the Lord one with us. We can see this in John 15.

The Lord Jesus was probably in a vineyard at the time He said this, and perhaps He found an attached branch that was all lying on the ground. It was probably dirty and muddy, and no sunlight could get to it. So no fruit was found on it. As He lifted it up, He started explaining how, after cleansing it and propping it up, it would begin producing fruit.

So it is with a lot of Christians who are down due to unbelief, condemnation, guilt, and shame, but after being cleaned up by the Word, they can see the Son of Righteousness, who will empower them to bear fruit. At the same time, every thought that does not match the kingdom mind-set He cuts off so we can be fruitful.

> *I am the true vine, and my Father is the husbandman. Every branch in me that beareth not fruit he taketh away: and every branch that beareth fruit, he purgeth it, that it may bring forth more fruit.*
>
> John 15:1–2

Abiding in or being one with Him in our minds causes us to bear much fruit, and that's how God gets the glory.

> *Now ye are clean through the word which I have spoken unto you. Abide in me, and I in you. As the branch cannot bear fruit of itself, except it abide in the vine; no more can ye, except ye abide in me. I am the vine, ye are the branches: He that abideth in me, and I in him, the same bringeth forth much fruit: for without me ye can do nothing. If a man abide not in me, he is cast forth as a branch, and is withered; and men gather them, and cast them into the fire, and they are burned. If ye abide in me, and my words abide in you, ye shall ask what ye will, and it shall be done unto you. Herein is my Father glorified, that ye bear much fruit; so shall ye be my disciples. As the Father hath loved me, so have I loved you: continue ye in my love.*
>
> John 15:3–9

Any teaching that speaks of our union with God will cause us to bear fruit, and the Father will get the glory. That teaching is of God. The teaching of separation from God is a demonic teaching because it robs us of fruit and robs God of glory.

Fruit is not for yourself, but rather for others to enjoy and for God to be glorified by.

> *I am the vine, ye are the branches: He that abideth in me, and I in him, the same bringeth forth much fruit: for without me ye can do nothing.*
>
> John 15:5

Abiding in Him does away with selfishness and self-sufficiency in your life. Abiding in your oneness with God fills you with His strength by aligning you with His heart. Abiding in your oneness with His Word makes your prayer a direct flow of His divine heart and will in every situation.

> *If ye abide in me, and my words abide in you, ye shall ask what ye will, and it shall be done unto you.*
>
> John 15:7

Abiding in our oneness with His love makes our joy full.

> *As the Father hath loved me, so have I loved you: continue ye in my love. If ye keep my commandments, ye shall abide in my love; even as I have kept my Father's commandments, and abide in his love. These things have I spoken unto you, that my joy might remain in you, and that your joy might be full.*
>
> John 15:9–11

In Matthew, there are two different words used in the Greek for "Peter": *Petros*, meaning "little rock," and *Petra*, meaning "huge rock." Therefore, what the Lord is really saying in the following verse is that He builds His church on the revelation that we are the little rocks, which are part of the huge rock, who is the Lord Jesus.

> *And I tell you that you are Peter, and on this rock I will build my church, and the gates of Hades will not overcome it.*
>
> Matthew 16:18

We are one with Him, born of the same Spirit, same word, and same love as our Lord Jesus.

Neither pray I for these alone, but for them also which shall believe on me through their word; That they all may be one; as thou, Father, art in me, and I in thee, that they also may be one in us: that the world may believe that thou hast sent me. And the glory which thou gavest me I have given them; that they may be one, even as we are one: I in them, and thou in me, that they may be made perfect in one; and that the world may know that thou hast sent me, and hast loved them, as thou hast loved me.

John 17:20–23

If we believe that the Lord's prayers were answered by the Father, if we believe that He had faith when He prayed, and if we believe that He spoke the truth when He prayed, then the only conclusion we can arrive at is that we are one with the Lord Jesus Christ and one with the Father, just as the Lord is one with the Father.

The Bible calls us the body of Christ, the bride of Christ, and the apple of His eye. I don't believe that these are just metaphors, but realities.

For as the body is one, and hath many members, and all the members of that one body, being many, are one body: so also is Christ. For by one Spirit are we all baptized into one body, whether we be Jews or Gentiles, whether we be bond or free; and have been all made to drink into one Spirit. For the body is not one member, but many.

1 Corinthians 12:12–14

This is a great mystery: but I speak concerning Christ and the church. Nevertheless let every one of you in particular so love his wife even as himself; and the wife see that she reverence her husband.

Ephesians 5:32–33

For thus saith the LORD of hosts; After the glory hath he sent me unto the nations which spoiled you: for he that toucheth you toucheth the apple of his eye.

Zechariah 2:8

CHAPTER 12

Giving and Generosity

There is so much misunderstanding in the body of Christ today about the subject of giving and being generous that I thought it needed to be included in this book. Hopefully, it will help shed some light on giving and generosity.

First, I'm all for giving and being generous in our giving, as I know what the Word of God says about how a generous person prospers.

> *A generous person will prosper; whoever refreshes others will be refreshed.*
>
> Proverbs 11:25

This is truth! If you are generous, you will prosper. However, many Christians allow guilt, condemnation, necessity, manipulation, and other people to dictate when they give, as well as how much they give. By doing this, they shut off the generosity of God within them, which is the very thing that stops them from prospering.

Let me disclose up front that when I say *giving*, I'm not only talking about money, although money is a big part of it in our day and time. Giving includes experience, teaching, knowledge, resources, time, effort, love, mercy, forgiveness, blessing, encouragement, instruction, gifts, and so much more.

Speaking of generosity, the first thing we need to know is that God is the most generous person in the universe and obviously the most prosperous person as well. Anyone that has anything good got it from Him, for He is the giver of *every* good and perfect gift, and He will continue to forever be.

> *Every good gift and every perfect gift is from above, and cometh down from the Father of lights, with whom is no variableness, neither shadow of turning.*
> James 1:17

God is also the most generous person in the entire universe because He doesn't give to get anything in return; He gives out of His very essence, which is love.

> *Or who hath first given to him, and it shall be recompensed unto him again? For of him, and through him, and to him, are all things: to whom be glory forever. Amen.*
> Romans 11:35–36

God is the most generous person because He gives unconditionally to His children as well as to those who consider themselves to be His enemies.

> *That ye may be the children of your Father which is in heaven: for he maketh his sun to rise on the evil and on the good, and sendeth rain on the just and on the unjust.*
> Matthew 5:45

God lives in all who have accepted Him as Lord and Savior and by virtue of same, His generous nature also abides in us. He wants this generosity to flow through us whenever there's an opportunity for it. The only issue is that many times we allow the law, religion, and other people to stop His generosity from being activated in our lives.

The law causes us to think that we *have* to give. Because of this, we won't be generous in our giving. Religion teaches us that we must give to get, thus trying to obtain our free inheritance in Jesus through what we do, rather than through what He did. We need to be careful not to allow other people to manipulate us by using guilt, condemnation, shame, greed, etc., to obtain things from us.

> *He who waters others shall be watered himself.*
> Proverbs 11:25

Giving should always be other-oriented, with no strings attached, done from a heart of love. For instance, in 2 Corinthians, we find that the Macedonians gave out of their deep poverty to help the saints in Jerusalem. The Corinthians gave for the benefit of the saints in Jerusalem, just as God gave Jesus for the benefit of us all. This is being other-oriented!

> *For ye know the grace of our Lord Jesus Christ, that,*
> *though he was rich, yet for your sakes he became poor,*
> *that ye through his poverty might be rich.*
> 2 Corinthians 8:9

What we see here is that giving involves grace and that the greatest seed ever planted for your prosperity is the Lord Jesus himself. Every blessing we receive from God, we receive because of our Lord

Jesus Christ and what He has done (we are coheirs with Christ) and not because of anything we do or don't do.

> *Now if we are children, then we are heirs—heirs of God and co-heirs with Christ, if indeed we share in his sufferings in order that we may also share in his glory.*
>
> Romans 8:17

When it comes to giving, one of the most important things is to trust God. I say this because the Lord Jesus taught about trusting God and not trusting anything else.

> *Behold the fowls of the air: for they sow not, neither do they reap, nor gather into barns; yet your heavenly Father feedeth them. Are ye not much better than they.*
>
> Matthew 6:26

In our vernacular, it would go something like this: Do not sow, do not reap (there goes the sowing and reaping, when it comes to giving), and do not save. Instead, trust God because you are more valuable than the birds to Him.

Here in this chapter, the Lord goes on to talk about trusting God or trusting mammon.

> *No man can serve two masters: for either he will hate the one, and love the other; or else he will hold to the one, and despise the other. Ye cannot serve God and mammon.*
>
> Matthew 6:34

Mammon could be anything or anybody we trust other than God. It could be the seed we sow, the faith we have, our possessions, parents, grandparents, career, job, business, savings, real estate investments, friends, spouse, or many other things. Our trust should be in God and Him alone, knowing that we have an immeasurable value in His eyes and that He loves us and cares deeply about each one of us.

I want to bring to your attention a few scriptures that have been taken out of context and misused to manipulate people into giving; I hope to bring some clarity. Let's look at Luke chapter 6:

In verse 30, the Lord talks about giving to a man who asks of you or takes from you.

> *Give to every man that asketh of thee; and of him that*
> *taketh away thy goods ask them not again.*

In verse 31, He tells us of the law of reciprocity among people.

> *And as ye would that men should do to you, do ye also*
> *to them likewise.*

In verse 32, He said we are to love every person, independent of his or her behavior. The encouragement here is to do good to all people, regardless of their behavior.

> *For if ye love them which love you, what thank have ye?*
> *for sinners also love those that love them.*

The lesson in verses 33–34 is that if you gave only to receive something back, why should anyone thank you.

> *And if ye do good to them which do good to you, what*
> *thank have ye? for sinners also do even the same. And*
> *if ye lend to them of whom ye hope to receive, what*

> *thank have ye? for sinners also lend to sinners, to receive as much again.*

In verse 35, we see that if you act based on the nature of God, you will have reward.

> *But love ye your enemies, and do good, and lend, hoping for nothing again; and your reward shall be great, and ye shall be the children of the Highest: for he is kind unto the unthankful and to the evil.*

In verse 36, you are to give mercy, for your Father from heaven is in you, and He is merciful.

> *Be ye therefore merciful, as your Father also is merciful.*

In verse 37, Jesus says we are not to pass judgment and to condemn, but rather to give forgiveness, and we shall receive forgiveness in return from people.

> *Judge not, and ye shall not be judged: condemn not, and ye shall not be condemned: forgive, and ye shall be forgiven.*

In all the giving mentioned above, money is not even mentioned. However, for the sake of it, let's say it applies. This does *not* say that *God* will give to you, but that *men* will give to you. Again, this is the law of reciprocity.

> *Give, and it shall be given unto you; good measure, pressed down, and shaken together, and running over, shall men give into your bosom. For with the same measure that ye mete withal it shall be measured to you again.*
>
> Luke 6:38

70

The following passage of scripture has been interpreted as saying that God will give you thirty-, sixty-, and a hundredfold.

> *Still other seed fell on good soil. It came up, grew and produced a crop, some multiplying thirty, some sixty, some a hundred times.*
>
> Mark 4:8

The Lord Jesus interpreted this parable for us, and He said that the seed is the Word of God, not money.

The apostle Paul didn't say to sow a seed in order meet your need or greed, but instead that God will meet your needs according to His riches in glory. See, it's not according to sowing, tithing, giving, good behavior, etc., but according to His riches in glory.

> *And my God will meet all your needs according to the riches of his glory in Christ Jesus.*
>
> Philippians 4:19

The following scripture is written to an Old Covenant people, and it is a common mistake to take it out of the context of that covenant, as has been done so many times, and interpreting it for us today.

> *Will a man rob God? Yet ye have robbed me. But ye say, wherein have we robbed thee? In tithes and offerings. Ye are cursed with a curse: for ye have robbed me, even this whole nation. Bring ye all the tithes into the storehouse, that there may be meat in mine house, and prove me now herewith, saith the LORD of hosts, if I will not open you the windows of heaven, and pour you out a blessing, that there shall not be room enough to receive it.*
>
> Malachi 3:8–10

I hope by now you know that we've been redeemed from the curse of the law.

> *Christ hath redeemed us from the curse of the law, being made a curse for us: for it is written, Cursed is every one that hangeth on a tree.*
>
> Galatians 3:13

We are married to Christ. How can you rob the one you are married to or the one you are a coheir with, the one who has already given us all things that pertain to life and godliness?

> *Wherefore, my brethren, ye also are become dead to the law by the body of Christ; that ye should be married to another, even to him who is raised from the dead, that we should bring forth fruit unto God.*
>
> Romans 7:4

> *And if children, then heirs; heirs of God, and joint-heirs with Christ; if so be that we suffer with him, that we may be also glorified together.*
>
> Romans 8:17

> *According as his divine power hath given unto us all things that pertain unto life and godliness, through the knowledge of him that hath called us to glory and virtue.*
>
> 2 Peter 1:3

> *He that spared not his own Son, but delivered him up for us all, how shall he not with him also freely give us all things?*
>
> Romans 8:32

To say God gave us Jesus but He will not give us all other things would be to say that God values money and other things more than his very own Son. We know that can't be true. The best thing about it all is that He shall freely give us all things. We get everything for free because of Jesus.

Second Corinthians 9:7 says,

> *Every man according as he purposeth in his heart, so let him give; not grudgingly, or of necessity: for God loveth a cheerful giver.*

Listen to how the Amplified Bible puts it:

> *Let each one give [thoughtfully and with purpose] just as he has decided in his heart, not grudgingly or under compulsion, for God loves a cheerful giver [and delights in the one whose heart is in his gift].*

Am I against giving? Of course not! To the contrary, I ask you to allow the generosity of God from within you to freely flow as the Lord Jesus lives in you. The only life He now lives is a life of generosity and giving.

CHAPTER 13

True Holiness

And be renewed in the spirit of your mind; And that
ye put on the new man, which after God is created in
righteousness and true holiness.

Ephesians 4:23–24

Holiness is the opposite of sin—not in our way of understanding it, but from God's view of holiness. In God's mind, holiness is sacred (set apart), meaning belonging to someone. In verse 24 above, we are told we were created in righteousness and true holiness. That means there is false holiness as well as true holiness. The false understanding of holiness is how religion interprets holiness, which is a standard of living that determines how we live, not our state of being.

Like I said, being truly holy means to be sacred, set apart unto someone. A great example is a married man. I am set apart for my wife, and she is set apart for me. The wedding ring is a symbol of holiness that reveals to the world that this one is set apart for someone. Obviously, belonging to my wife transforms the way I live and the way she lives as well.

Likewise, understanding that we belong (are holy, set apart) to God transforms the way we live once we understand and believe this truth.

> *Because it is written, be ye holy; for I am holy.*
>
> 1 Peter 1:16

This seems to be a command according to this translation, but let's look at the Interlinear Version, which translates it word for word from Greek:

> *Because it has been written, holy you will be for I holy am.*

The meaning totally changes in the Interlinear, showing us that this verse is not a command but rather a promise: "You will belong to Me because I belong to you."

One day I asked the Lord, "why did you ask Moses to remove his shoes at the burning bush in Exodus 3?"

The Lord replied, "Why do you remove your shoes when you get home?"

I answered, "Because I know that I belong there, that I can rest, and that I'm not going anywhere anytime soon."

The Lord said, "That's exactly what I wanted to convey to Moses at that time."

As I thought about this, I realized that the land didn't become holy because Moses removed his shoes, but because God's presence was there. In the same way, we do not become holy by what we do but by the One we belong to.

This understanding of holiness should bring peace and comfort to our hearts and minds. It should allow us to fellowship freely with God, knowing we are fully accepted, unconditionally loved and, more than anything, that this is the great desire that made Him sacrifice Himself just to be with us.

The direct result of embracing this understanding of holiness is that it totally and effortlessly transforms our lives to the extent that people around us notice the transformation. The alternative is to live in fear and separation from God and in a mind-set of performance, which produces fear, lack of fruitfulness, and torment, thinking we aren't measuring up. For those that still want this alternative, I ask these questions:

- ➢ When is it enough?
- ➢ When are we qualified?
- ➢ What is the standard?
- ➢ When are we good enough?

If the answer to these is "I don't know," I suggest that you relax and enjoy God. Give Him a try, and don't worry. After all, you can always go back to the old way if you don't like relaxing and living without worry.

I embraced this new understanding twenty-seven years ago, and I never went back to a performance mentality. The new way of grace can never be compared to the old understanding.

CHAPTER 14

The Fear of God

H ere's the million-dollar question that many ask: does fear originate from God, or is it evil? This question definitely needs to be answered because many believers are confused about this subject and are trying to get an answer that will help them understand who God is and how He rules His creation. Does He rule by fear and intimidation, or does He rule by love and grace?

Let's looks at the origin of fear.

> *And he said, I heard thy voice in the garden, and I was afraid, because I was naked; and I hid myself.*
> Genesis 3:10

We can see here that fear appeared for the first time in Genesis, right after Adam and Eve sinned. Fear is a result of sin. It doesn't have its origin in God. Hundreds of times in scripture we find God saying, "Do not be afraid" or "Fear not." Therefore, it's not even a possibility that God would rule His creation by fear and intimidation. Instead, it's very clear that God is love, so the way He rules is by His love, giving His creation the right to choose.

Beloved, let us love one another: for love is of God; and every one that loveth is born of God, and knoweth God. He that loveth not knoweth not God; for God is love. In this was manifested the love of God toward us, because that God sent his only begotten Son into the world, that we might live through Him. Herein is love, not that we loved God, but that He loved us, and sent His Son to be the propitiation for our sins.

1 John 4:7–10

Not only is God love, but this text clearly states that love is *of* God, meaning it has its origin in God and is manifested toward us in the fact that God sent His only begotten Son into the world that we might live through Him.

For God hath not given us the spirit of fear; but of power, and of love, and of a sound mind.

2 Timothy 1:7

God didn't give us the spirit of fear, for He never intended for us to experience fear. The truth is that we experience fear only when we feel powerless or unloved, or when our thinking is unsound. People are not afraid of something scary; they are afraid of what that something or someone could do to them.

There is no fear in love. But perfect love drives out fear, because fear has to do with punishment. The one who fears is not made perfect in love.

1 John 4:18 NIV

God is love so that means there is no fear in God. At the same time, believing in the perfect love of God for you will eradicate fear from your life. You might be asking, "What about fearing God?" as mentioned in this verse:

> *The fear of the Lord is the beginning of wisdom, and knowledge of the holy one is understanding.*
>
> Proverbs 9:10

The meaning of *fear* in this verse is obviously reverence toward God or amazement about who He is. This reverence and/or amazement causes you to want to get closer to Him and to learn more from Him. This is *not* a fear that would cause you to run and hide from Him, thinking He wants to punish you.

One of the things I do as a pastor is counsel a lot of people. In one of my counseling sessions, a man asked that I give him some biblical advise. After listening to him, I knew that he was dealing with a lot of fear and torment, especially fear of God and of going to hell.

As I always like to do, I brought a second person into the session with me, and we found out that the fear this man was experiencing was so advanced that the minute we got to talking about God, and especially certain passages from the book of Hebrews (such as Hebrews 6—10), the fear manifested in uncontrolled shaking.

After explaining Hebrews 6, we came to agreement that it doesn't apply to believers until you get down to verse 9. This is where Paul started addressing believers, using the word *beloved*.

> *But, beloved, we are persuaded better things of you, and things that accompany salvation, though we thus speak.*
>
> Hebrews 6:9

I moved on to chapter 10 and explained how the sacrifice and the blood of Jesus are far superior to those of bulls and goats. I further explained that willful sin in this passage referred to someone that, after accepting our Lord Jesus and His supreme and perfect sacrifice, decided that the sacrifice of Jesus was not enough and therefore wanted to bring a blood sacrifice of an animal to gain entrance into the presence of God or to find acceptance before God. That act would be the trampling of the blood of Jesus underfoot, which would be despising the Spirit of grace.

Nevertheless, he asked, "So you say that by my going and sleeping around after receiving Jesus was not trampling His blood under my feet?"

I responded with one question: "Are you telling me that by sleeping around with someone, you brought another sacrifice to God?"

"No, how can you even say that?"

"So you agree that through what you did, you did not actually bring another sacrifice to God to gain entrance into God's presence, right?"

"Right, I did not."

"Then this text does not apply to you."

Fear and torment left this person because we had cut fear's legs off; it no longer had a leg to stand on. The truth had set this one free. Hallelujah!

> *For by one offering he hath perfected forever them that are sanctified.*
>
> Hebrews 10:14

For if we sin willfully after that we have received the knowledge of the truth, there remaineth no more sacrifice for sins, but a certain fearful looking for of judgment and fiery indignation, which shall devour the adversaries. He that despised Moses' law died without mercy under two or three witnesses: of how much sorer punishment, suppose ye, shall he be thought worthy, who hath trodden under foot the Son of God, and hath counted the blood of the covenant, wherewith he was sanctified, an unholy thing, and hath done despite unto the spirit of grace?

Hebrews 10:26–29

Maybe you have been tormented by fear because of not having a right understanding of these passages of scripture. Hopefully you are open enough to the truth that when you know it, it sets you free.

CHAPTER **15**

The Covenant of God with Humanity

I realize that a lot of the things I wrote in this book about God and His relationship with us may have raised questions in your mind. I want to take some time to answer two of the most common questions I receive from people as I teach in various places about the goodness, the lovingkindness, and the grace of God.

First Question

"How about the God of the Old Testament?"

Unless and until we understand the teachings on God's various covenants with us, we will never be able to understand why God did what He did and why He related to people the way He did in the Old Testament.

There are five different covenants that God had with mankind, which are as follows:

THE COVENANT OF GOD WITH NOAH

*I establish my covenant with you: Never again will all
life be destroyed by the waters of a flood; never again
will there be a flood to destroy the earth.*

Genesis 9:11 NIV

THE COVENANT OF GOD WITH ABRAHAM

*Now the Lord had said unto Abram, Get thee out
of thy country, and from thy kindred, and from thy
father's house, unto a land that I will shew thee:
And I will make of thee a great nation, and I will
bless thee, and make thy name great; and thou shalt
be a blessing: And I will bless them that bless thee,
and curse him that curseth thee: and in thee shall all
families of the earth be blessed.*

Genesis 12:1–3

THE COVENANT OF GOD WITH MOSES

*Ye have seen what I did unto the Egyptians, and how
I bare you on eagles' wings, and brought you unto
myself. Now therefore, if ye will obey my voice indeed,
and keep my covenant, then ye shall be a peculiar
treasure unto me above all people: for all the earth is
mine: and ye shall be unto me a kingdom of priests,
and an holy nation. These are the words which thou
shalt speak unto the children of Israel.*

Exodus 19:4–6 AKJV

THE COVENANT OF GOD WITH DAVID

When your days are complete and you lie down with your fathers, I will raise up your descendant after you, who will come forth from you, and I will establish his kingdom. He shall build a house for My name, and I will establish the throne of his kingdom forever. I will be a father to him and he will be a son to Me; when he commits iniquity, I will correct him with the rod of men and the strokes of the sons of men, but My lovingkindness shall not depart from him, as I took it away from Saul, whom I removed from before you. Your house and your kingdom shall endure before Me forever; your throne shall be established forever. In accordance with all these words and all this vision, so Nathan spoke to David.

2 Samuel 7:12–17 NASB

THE COVENANT OF GOD WITH OUR LORD JESUS

Behold, the days come, saith the Lord, that I will make a new covenant with the house of Israel, and with the house of Judah: not according to the covenant that I made with their fathers in the day that I took them by the hand to bring them out of the land of Egypt; which my covenant they brake, although I was an husband unto them, saith the Lord: but this shall be the covenant that I will make with the house of Israel; After those days, saith the Lord, I will put my law in their inward parts, and write it in their hearts; and will be their God, and they shall be my people. And they shall teach no more every man his neighbour,

*and every man his brother, saying, know the Lord:
for they shall all know me, from the least of them unto
the greatest of them, saith the Lord: for I will forgive
their iniquity, and I will remember their sin no more.*
Jeremiah 31:31–34 AKJV

*In the same way, after the supper he took the cup,
saying, "This cup is the new covenant in my blood,
which is poured out for you."*
Luke 22:20 NIV

GRANT COVENANTS

Four of these five covenants listed above are grant covenants, meaning everything in them is granted by God; He assumes the whole responsibility for the fulfilment of those covenants. If there is any contribution on our side, His divine influence would take care of that.

VASSAL COVENANTS

The term *vassal covenant* goes back to a time when a king would make a promise to his subjects, or would make a treaty with other kings, that depended on obedience to specific terms. You can think of this covenant as a conditional promise.

As opposed to a vassal covenant, a grant covenant requires no action on the part of the beneficiary. It is an unconditional promise granted from one party to another.

The one covenant that does not fall in this category is the covenant God had with Moses, the Mosaic covenant. This covenant is a kingship covenant that later turned into a vassal covenant.

KINGSHIP COVENANTS

At Mount Sinai, God intended to give the people of Israel a grant covenant, but they asked for a kingship covenant instead. You might ask, "What's the difference?" In a kingship covenant, there is a treaty, which in the case of Israel were the Ten Commandments. The two kings would say that, unless we abide by this treaty, our God will punish us, and our covenant partner will go to war with the other partner anytime it's needed. This explains why God punished people in the Old Covenant and why He went to war with them, thus killing for them. By way of the kingship covenant, this is explicitly what they asked for. God's desire was to be with them, and if that meant He would have to come down to their level, that's what He did.

As we can see from the following scripture in Matthew, our Lord Jesus is presenting God's true nature, clearly showing us that in the Old Covenant, God came down to our level, but in the New Covenant, we are shown clearly who and what God is really like.

> *Ye have heard that it hath been said, Thou shalt love thy neighbour, and hate thine enemy. But I say unto you, Love your enemies, bless them that curse you, do good to them that hate you, and pray for them which despitefully use you, and persecute you; That ye may be the children of your Father which is in heaven: for he maketh his sun to rise on the evil and on the good, and sendeth rain on the just and on the unjust. For if*

*ye love them which love you, what reward have ye? do
not even the publicans the same? And if ye salute your
brethren only, what do ye more than others? do not
even the publicans so? Be ye therefore perfect, even as
your Father which is in heaven is perfect.*

Matthew 5:43–48

Second Question

The second question that I am often asked is *"What about the wrath
of God in the book of Revelation?"* First of all, scripture clearly tells
us that the law is what brought the wrath of God.

*Because the law worketh wrath: for where no law is,
there is no transgression.*

Romans 4:15 KJV

In Revelation 15, we see that the wrath of God completed, meaning
there is no more wrath left. If we connect this passage with the
destruction of Jerusalem in AD 70, then when the Mosaic covenant
was destroyed, the wrath of God was completed.

*I saw in heaven another great and marvelous sign:
seven angels with the seven last plagues—last, because
with them God's wrath is completed.*

Revelation 15:1

The covenant of God with our Lord Jesus is a covenant of
unconditional love, forgiveness, acceptance, and goodness wherein
the true nature of God is on full display. The Lord Jesus is the
perfect representation of God to us, Him being the brightness of
God's glory and the express image of God's person.

God, who at sundry times and in divers manners spake in time past unto the fathers by the prophets, hath in these last days spoken unto us by his Son, whom he hath appointed heir of all things, by whom also he made the worlds; who being the brightness of his glory, and the express image of his person, and upholding all things by the word of his power, when he had by himself purged our sins, sat down on the right hand of the Majesty on high.

Hebrews 1:1–3 AKJV

CHAPTER 16

The Authority of the Scriptures

In this book, I used a lot of scriptures. I have done it for a purpose: to have the authority needed that is received through the scriptures, which are inspired by God. I believe that if there is any transformation that will occur in anyone's life, it comes as a result of the revelation given by the Holy Spirit through the holy and inspired scriptures.

As I minister to people, I'm very aware of the truth that God has decided to speak to us through the scriptures and that through them we can get to know the living Word, who is the Lord Jesus Himself, as well as to know God the Father and God the Holy Spirit. I am all for sharing with each other our experiences we each have with the Lord, but all that we experience needs to be filtered through the scriptures to prevent us from ending up in some sort of error, relying more on our experiences than we do on the scriptures.

And that from a child thou hast known the holy scriptures, which are able to make thee wise unto salvation through faith which is in Christ Jesus. All scripture is given by inspiration of God, and is

> *profitable for doctrine, for reproof, for correction, for*
> *instruction in righteousness: that the man of God may*
> *be perfect, thoroughly furnished unto all good works.*
>
> 2 Timothy 3:15–17 AKJV

Here in these verses, we find the truth that all scripture is holy. It is inspired by God (God-breathed), meaning that God wanted all that is written in the Bible to be included therein and that all scripture is profitable for teaching us about who God is and about who we are. It also reproves us or proves to us again and again the truth about who we are in Him, His view of us, and His love for us.

The scriptures are also needed to correct us whenever we start thinking God is not a good and loving God, full of compassion and mercy, abounding in goodness and truth. It also corrects us whenever we start thinking about ourselves in a way that does not fit God's heart and mind for us. Whenever we do not see ourselves as holy, righteous, redeemed, cleansed, forgiven, accepted, beloved, good, merciful, joyful, blessed, etc., it's time for us to remind ourselves of this truth through the scriptures.

The scriptures are to be used for instruction in righteousness (restoration) and not for condemnation. This is the way a man or woman of God may be perfect and fully equipped for every good work.

> *Study to shew thyself approved unto god, a workman*
> *that needeth not to be ashamed, rightly dividing the*
> *word of truth.*
>
> 2 Timothy 2:15 KJV

In this verse, we see Paul writing to Timothy about the purpose for which we should study the scriptures. It is obvious that there are many Christians who study the scriptures for all the wrong reasons. "Study to show thyself approved unto God" means that the primary purpose of studying the scriptures is to show and prove to ourselves the fact that we are approved of God. We aren't supposed to show this truth to God, for God already approves of us. But our hearts need convincing; our hearts need to be reaffirmed in this truth; our hearts need to be told again and again the truth that we are accepted by God.

Our hearts need to be convinced that we have no reason to be ashamed because Jesus took all our shame away when He, the Lamb of God, took the sins of the world away. It is only when we realize that we are accepted by God and that we have no reason to be ashamed that we are rightly dividing the Word of Truth.

You've probably heard the saying "I will tell them the truth in love," meaning I will let them know how wrong they are in certain situations. In doing this, people think they're helping others; however, let us see what the scriptures say about sharing the truth in love.

> *In whom ye also trusted, after that ye heard the word*
> *of truth, the gospel of your salvation: in whom also*
> *after that ye believed, ye were sealed with that holy*
> *spirit of promise.*
>
> Ephesians 1:13 KJV

According to this scripture, the truth about someone is the gospel, or the good news, about his or her salvation, and after believing in God, that person was sealed by the Holy Spirit of God. The scriptures point us to the living Word of God.

> *Search the scriptures; for in them ye think ye have*
> *eternal life: and they are they which testify of me.*
>
> John 5:39 KJV

Jesus is saying basically that eternal life is in Him, and not in the scriptures themselves, but that the scriptures point us to Him. So one of the main purposes of scripture is to point us to the Lord Jesus Christ who is the living Word of God.

> *Therefore, beloved, looking forward to these things, be diligent to be found by Him in peace, without spot and blameless; and consider that the longsuffering of our Lord is salvation—as also our beloved brother Paul, according to the wisdom given to him, has written to you, as also in all his epistles, speaking in them of these things, in which are some things hard to understand, which untaught and unstable people twist to their own destruction, as they do also the rest of the scriptures.*
> 2 Peter 3:14–16 NKJV

In verse 16 of this passage, we find the apostle Peter equating the writings of the apostle Paul to the scriptures of the Old Testament, thus qualifying the Epistles of Paul as scriptures. There is one thing we need to understand: all scripture is holy, all scripture is God-breathed, and all scripture is useful to us. However, also in the scriptures we find men's distorted opinion about God or other matters. Although it is an accurate recording and was intended by God to be included in the scriptures, there are passages in which we see different people's opinions about God.

Here is a famous scripture from the book of Job that is often misunderstood:

> *And said: "naked I came from my mother's womb, and naked I will depart. The Lord gave and the Lord has taken away; may the name of the Lord be praised."*
> Job 1:21 NIV

In this verse we find Job's opinion about what happened in his life. However, we know that it is not God that takes away; it is the devil.

Job's opinions, as well as the opinions of some of Job's friends, are not what God said but what people said. Therefore, we can't take those opinions and teach out of them, because we would be in error.

If we want to always understand the heart and mind of God, it is of the essence that we look at Jesus and everything He taught us and learn to filter all scripture through His life, character, and teachings, as He is the perfect and complete representation of our heavenly Father.

> *God, who at sundry times and in divers manners spake in time past unto the fathers by the prophets, hath in these last days spoken unto us by His Son, whom He hath appointed heir of all things, by whom also He made the worlds; who being the brightness of His glory, and the express image of His person, and upholding all things by the word of his power, when he had by himself purged our sins, sat down on the right hand of the majesty on high.*
>
> Hebrews 1:1–3 KJV

CONCLUSION

I leave you with the truth that however and whatever our view of God is, that's ultimately the way we live out our lives. The revelation we have about who God is will be reflected in our daily lives. Whatever manner it is that we believe God relates to us, will in turn be the very same way we are going to relate to our families, our friends, and all with whom we come in contact with.

In him was life; and the life was the light of men.

John 1:4 AKJV

Hopefully, after reading this book, your view of God is that He is extremely good, unconditionally and relentlessly loving, abundantly rich in mercy and grace, full of compassion, full of wisdom, having all knowledge, and having the best intentions of all time for you.

For I know the thoughts that I think toward you, saith the Lord, thoughts of peace, and not of evil, to give you an expected end.

Jeremiah 29:11 AKJV

I'm also expecting that your view of yourself has been transformed into that of a beloved of God, a person designed to live in the presence of God, a man or woman of extreme value in the eyes of God, independent of your performance, released into a life marked by unconditional, other-oriented, self-sacrificial love that flows like a river from deep within your willing heart, for the purpose of bringing life and restoration to all that have been hurt in different ways while living here on this earth. I hope you can allow the atmosphere, love, and light of heaven to penetrate this physical realm you live in and overthrow whatever selfishness, hate, fear, and/or darkness that has surrounded you in times past.

> For as he thinketh in his heart, so is he: Eat and drink, saith he to thee; but his heart is not with thee.
>
> Proverbs 23:7

Lastly, I hope that you can clearly see that the devil has been defeated, thrown out, stripped of all power, having only one thing left: the demonic system of religion through which he still tries to create chaos in the lives of so many people.

Understanding and believing this truth will set you free from fear and will empower you to fulfill the destiny God has prepared for you to walk in.

> And again, I will put my trust in him. And again, Behold I and the children which God hath given me. Forasmuch then as the children are partakers of flesh and blood, he also himself likewise took part of the same; that through death he might destroy him that had the power of death, that is, the devil; And deliver them who through fear of death were all their lifetime subject to bondage.
>
> Hebrews 2:13–15

This book would not be complete without giving you an opportunity to begin fellowshipping with this amazing God who is longing for you and desires to share His life with you and give you happiness for the rest of the days of your earthly life and for all eternity. If this is what your heart is desiring, please pray this prayer:

> Lord God, thank You for loving me, creating me, and saving me. Thank You for making me a part of Your great family. I want to know You and the plans and purposes for which You created me. In Jesus's name, I thank You, Lord.

> *How blessed is God! And what a blessing he is! He's the Father of our Master, Jesus Christ, and takes us to the high places of blessing in him. Long before he laid down earth's foundations, he had us in mind, had settled on us as the focus of his love, to be made whole and holy by his love. Long, long ago he decided to adopt us into his family through Jesus Christ. (What pleasure he took in planning this!) He wanted us to enter into the celebration of his lavish gift-giving by the hand of his beloved Son.*
>
> Ephesians 1:3–6

If you've been blessed and your life has been changed by reading this book, if your view of God has been transformed, and equally as important, if your view of yourself has been transformed, and you would like to share this transformation with me, your feedback is most welcomed. You can email your response to johnblig@gmail.com. Additionally, if you would like to hear my sermons, please go to our church website listed below. You can also like and follow us on Facebook.

John Blig
Senior Pastor
Oasis of Light Church
San Antonio, Texas
www.theoasisoflight.org
facebook.com/oasisoflightchurch

Printed in the United States
By Bookmasters